Maurice Baxter

St Christopher with psalm and song

Maurice Baxter

St Christopher with psalm and song

ISBN/EAN: 9783741163869

Manufactured in Europe, USA, Canada, Australia, Japa

Cover: Foto ©Lupo / pixelio.de

Manufactured and distributed by brebook publishing software (www.brebook.com)

Maurice Baxter

St Christopher with psalm and song

ST. CHRISTOPHER,

WITH

PSALM AND SONG.

BY

MAURICE BAXTER,
Author of
" JAMES STRATHGELD, PART OF AN AUTOBIOGRAPHY."

London:
HODDER AND STOUGHTON,
PATERNOSTER ROW.
MDCCCLXXVI.

CONTENTS.

PAGE

MONOLOGUES.
    I. St. Christopher   11
    II. A Wise Virgin   17
    III. A Foolish Virgin   19
    IV. St. Peter   21
    V. St. John   24
    VI. St. Thomas   26

DIALOGUES.
    I. The Temptation   33
    II. A Fine Sunday   42
    III. Law and Liberty   46

PSALM AND SONG.

	PAGE
A GIFT	55
"SUFFER LITTLE CHILDREN"	57
"WHAT THINK YE OF CHRIST?"	59
THE WORD OF THE LORD	63
MORNING	65
EVENING I.	67
„ II.	68
ADVENT I.	71
„ II.	73
„ III.	74
CHRISTMAS	76
FOR LENT	79
PALM SUNDAY	81
GOOD FRIDAY	84
EASTER	87
ASCENSION-DAY	89
WHITSUNDAY	92
TRINITY SUNDAY	94
A CHILD'S MORNING HYMN	97
A CHILD'S CHRISTMAS CAROL	99
BAPTISM	103

Contents.

	PAGE
HOLY COMMUNION I.	105
,, II.	106
CHRISTIAN MISSIONS	108
THE BUILDING OF A NEW CHURCH	111
THE POOL OF BETHESDA	114
FOR THOSE AT SEA IN STORM	116
THE SOWER	118
THE BURDEN-BEARER	120
EMMAUS	122
THE ATONEMENT	125
THE GOODLY FELLOWSHIP OF THE PROPHETS	127
THE IDEAL TEMPLE	129
THE GOOD SHEPHERD	131
THE UNIVERSAL FATHER	134
THE WATCHFUL PROVIDENCE	137
THE ETERNAL PRESENCE	139
THE NEW WORLD	142
FOR TIME OF TEMPTATION	145
FOR TIME OF SICKNESS	148
FOR THE HOUR OF DEATH	150

MONOLOGUES.

I.

ST. CHRISTOPHER.

OFTTIMES I see a silver Christ in dreams,
Again I hear a sound of rushing streams,
With the harsh creaking of the wind-tossed pine;
Whilst with uncertain smile a faint moonshine
Breaks through the black rents of the flying storm,
And glistens on a little patient form;—
A young child waiting in the blast and rain;
Hark! through the pauses of the wind again,
That unknown cry of "Christopher" comes clear;—
But, children, gather round, and you shall hear.

Almighty God has built me tall and strong,
To Him alone these giant limbs belong.
But once in turn I served each warrior lord,
The weak deserting for the rising sword.
In the brown East, amidst the wastes of sand,
I heard the story of a western land,
Where all is oasis, for Christ is King;
Where naught is barren, for the deserts sing;
As "King of kings" they cried His regal fame,
And so to offer sword and suit I came.

But never Christian folk had seen His face,
They all were busy seeking pelf or place.
The priest, the shepherd of the worldly fold,
Alone the wondrous vision could behold.
The priest bemoaned his lack of time to look,
For he was searching for a bishop's crook,
But bade me to the hermit, dwelling high
Above the noisy world and near the sky;
Perchance the face of God, the vision sealed,
In mountain solitudes might be revealed.

St. Christopher.

Deep in the cloister shadow of the pine,
Where incense rises from each stately line,
The hermit dwelt, and offered worship there;
Haggard he was from fast and midnight prayer;
Yet once that withered face and shrunken form
Was lusty with a youth and vigour warm.
When lo! the Church proclaimed "The Lord is near,
With vengeance on the world will He appear.
Leave father, mother; dead must bury dead;
Flee to the mountain,"—and anon he fled.

" A rugged road, my son," the hermit cried,
" To reach the vision of the Crucified.
By frequent fast the veil of sense grows dim—
Upon the crucifix I gaze on Him,
Until the mournful visage seems to glow,
The eyes to shine, soft breath to come and go.
Prostrate I fall, and sight and hearing strain,
Some revelation of my Lord to gain;
But not a whispered word has reached my ears,
For half a century of prayers and tears."

Whilst as he spoke the mountain torrent roared,
There came a cry from pilgrims at the ford,
Where with the waxing year the waters rose,
Fed with the summer waste of Alpine snows.
" Father, whilst you remain to fast and pray,
Bid me assist the pilgrims on their way.
Sturdy in limb I am, in 'paters' slow;
Each with the best of gifts to Christ should go;
Upon His altar rest your fast and prayer,
Humbly I lay my strength of manhood there."

No longer was the ford a pilgrims' grave;
For many a day I dared the mountain wave,
Until the summer waned and woods were dumb,
The bees were silenced, and the insect hum.
From autumn boughs streamed banners red and gold,
Earth's beauty passed again, a tale twice told;
Among the boughs the glacier winds made moan;
The pine branch shed its rough and fretted cone,
And not a spike of quick and vivid green
About its grave and ghostly garb was seen.

St. Christopher.

And so it fell upon a stormy night,
When wind and rain had lashed the waters white,
Whene'er the storm drew breath I heard again
A young voice ring, for which I sought in vain,
Until the moon with momentary gleam
Revealed a little child beside the stream.
With lifted hands my pity he implored,
And prayed me bear him safely o'er the ford;
In vain I pictured all the night's alarms,
So raised the burden lightly in my arms.

But as I stemmed the wave, the trifling weight
Became a load intolerably great.
The awful burden pressed me fainting down,
The savage waters leaped with zest to drown;
And when I gained the shore, with battle wild,
I only cast to ground a little child.
"O child!" but speech was silenced in surprise,
For what a sudden glory met my eyes:
That little form was glowing more and more,
With silver light no moon e'er gave before.

Around His head the shining mists did float,
Bestud with orient pearls His dewy coat;
The tender radiance streaming from His face
Transformed with summer twilight all the place.
"Christ bearer, Christopher, thy name shalt be,
Thy love for little ones was love for Me.
Earth's sin and sorrow thy brave shoulders bore
In those brief moments bearing Me to shore."
He spoke; He passed away; now all is told.
Yet, children, here I stay, though growing old.

II.

A WISE VIRGIN.

I HEARD the voice sound through the night,
    I woke to see the Bridegroom's face;
My lamp, Thy gift to me, was bright,
    And since I brought a little light,
Thy hand has led me to this place,
    To view this goodly shining sight.

The waiting was so long and drear,
    My watching eyelids wearied fell;
Now all is past and Thou art near,
    The outer dark I do not fear,
And I that wondrous love will tell
    Which set me to these dainties here.

A Wise Virgin.

But lo! a wailing breaks our song,
    We hear a sobbing at the gate;
It is the five who did the wrong,
    To whom no entrance can belong,
But still they disbelieve, they wait,
    They think to join the wedding throng.

The door is closed, they beat in vain;
    'Tis at the Bridegroom's heart they cry;
Though sad, He will not spare their pain,
    But dying, they will live again,
The great Refiner standing by,
    Will purge the dross, the gold to gain.

I do not dare for them to plead,
    Thy wounds, five earnest voices, pray;
The Son of man, who once could bleed,
    With Son of God will intercede,
As man with God till dawn of day
    Strove and prevailed on Jabbok's mead.

III.

A FOOLISH VIRGIN.

LORD, light, light, the stars have all burnt out,
    The star of Jacob fails in blackest cloud,
My lamp is dead, so blind and full of doubt,
    I, groping for the door, cry out aloud,
        There is all light within,
        But here all dark and sin.
    I know Thee, Lord, reach out and take me in.

" Not Thine—I never loved Thee," yea, I know
    I did not kneel on Zion's blood-stained steep,
So I must learn from Sinai's fiery brow,
    And turning back to tremble and to weep,

Through painful wandering,
Must feel the serpent's sting,
Must cool my tongue at Marah's bitter spring.

Remember, Lord, how in the midday dark,
  That Thou didst seek in vain Thy Father's face,
And give to me one burning, shining spark,
  To dwell within, and lead through wrath to grace;
    So like the desert tree,
    My patient soul shall be
Wrapt round with flame, yet not consumed by Thee.

Thy feet are wet with sinful women's tears;
  The crown of gold Thy bleeding brows have dimmed;
And can the toiling of Thy thirty years
  Be satisfied with songs the wise have hymned;
    Whilst other sheep there are,
    And one fold, wilt Thou bar?
    And shall loud weeping the hosannas mar?

IV.

ST. PETER.

"Thou art Peter, and upon this rock," &c.

NO rock was I, but fickle sea;
   My heart a wanton Galilee,
Now slumbering 'neath a silver haze,
Now buoyant with the mountain breeze,
But swift to change with darkening days,
To fret and toss with angry seas;
Inconstant, passionate, and yet
Within this heart I cast my net,
With anxious toil some good to find,
Dark nights I spent in toiling vain,

St. Peter.

Till suddenly this barren main,
Teemed under Thy direction kind.

No rock was I, but troubled wave;—
I thought the raging storm to brave,
I thought to walk the midnight sea,
Thy path to prison and to death,
With storm-tossed soul I followed Thee,
Denying with my failing breath.
O gentle look that memory pained!
O gracious hand that life sustained!
O blessed voice the storm that stilled!
Across my soul Thy footsteps pass,
And calm it to a sea of glass,
A crystal rock on which to build.

If rock am I, 'tis of Thy grace,
And I will take the lowest place;
Who lays foundations firm and sure,
Contented toils unseen, unknown,
And when Thy Church's columns soar,

St. Peter.

No voice shall praise the hidden stone;
In gospels sent to distant lands,
The frail denying Peter stands,
No future gospel shall proclaim
My care Thy parting charge to keep,
To feed Thy scattered lambs and sheep,
My coming martyrdom and shame.

V.

ST. JOHN.*

HAST thou no crown of martyrdom for me?
   For Peter hangs upon his Master's tree,
The sword for James, and life for John alone,
Bleached column on a plain with ruins strown?
Thou doest well although I tarry long,
For many Judases their Lord betray,
And I alone can stem the doubting throng
Who wrest Thy Godhead and Thy rank away,
And this is martyrdom from day to day.

* The ordinary Ephesian tradition of St. John is here followed.

St. John.

Have I not leaned the nearest to Thy breast,
And known its beating tenderness the best?
And on the mountain in transforming light
Heard the strange voice and seen Thy garments white.
Long in my heart the treasured memory lay,
Now for Thine honour's sake I break the seal;—
My burning spirit will not brook delay,
Answer these scoffers in Thy thunder peal!
Nay, through my lips their God of love reveal.

Now I have spoken, now am old and worn;
Apocalyptic heights my feet have trod,
And exile paths; these wearied eyes have borne
Your awful glow, O jewelled streets of God.
Lord, Peter's word, "And what shall this man do?"
Answer Thy servant not in trumpet tone,
Nor in a burning form appear in view,
Girdled about the paps with golden zone,
Lest at Thy feet again I fall as dead,
But on Thy bosom bid me rest my head.

VI.

ST. THOMAS.*

BROTHER, when I saw Thee lowly,
   In our home at Nazareth,
Could I have foreseen the holy
Triumph of Thy life and death?
Joining in humble village toil
At the same bench were workers twain,
But Thy pure soul received no stain,
Only on me came labour's soil.

* The tradition is here adopted that Thomas belonged to the family of Jesus Christ.

St. Thomas.

       Brother and Friend,
River of God Thou living source,
Traced I not Thy fruitful course.
I thought the stream in Nazareth would spend,
A mountain valley's verdure seemed its end.

Master, unto John's baptizing,
Sought we Jordan's tawny stream,
From the sacred wave arising,
Now no brother didst Thou seem,
Parted from me, from man removed,
Living in desert's solitude,
Midst stocks and stones and creatures rude,
Thy true Messiahship was proved.
       Master and King,
I beheld Thy new-born power,
Born in dark temptation's hour,
How to Thy skirts the sick and sorry cling,
And tribute—sins and sores—the people bring.

Master, with the few believing
Of Thy faithless family,
I was of the band receiving
Gifts of healing ministry.
Dead men arose to swell Thy train,
Sick and possessed Thy word set free,
Joined in the mighty company
Who shouted, "Take Thy power and reign."

    Master, Thy sway
Ended in the garden grave,
Saviour with no power to save,
Mighty Messiah, who must death obey,
Where didst Thou go? how could we know the way?

Master, hear my interceding
For my long undying race;
Every age shall need my pleading,
Doubting souls in every place;
Loving the Christ whom once they hold,
Faithful to death, if faithful found,
Their faith in sensuous fetters bound,

St. Thomas.

They walk apart, distrustful, cold.
      Saviour and God,
As to me Thyself reveal,
Bid them stretch their hands and feel,
Then with faith's resurrection from the sod,
Bursts from them, "Brother, Master, Lord, and God."

DIALOGUES.

I.

THE TEMPTATION.

"And the devil said unto him, If thou be the Son of God."

I.

The Wilderness.

Christ. My Father, I am with Thee still,
    But in my soul Thine accents cease,
    And now the forty days of peace
Have yielded to a dread of ill.
The senses chained resume their reign,
    And from these rugged heights descending,
The haunts of man I seek again,
    A greater Moses Thou art sending

From converse with Thee on the Mount,
Thy newer message to recount.
'Tis past—that dawn of hope with fears,
   Thy Son in doubtless daylight stands;
He felt in early childhood's years
   The claiming touches of Thy hands.
Thy Godhead in Him 'gan to stir,
   And drove Him forth from Mary's cot,
Nor yet He dare the truth aver,
   And yet but dimly guessed His lot,
Until a dovelike One appearing,
Proclaimed Him in the Baptist's hearing,
And all on Jordan's crowded mead
Heard He was Son of God indeed.

Satan (appearing as a Jewish Rabbi).
Well met! disciple young and warm,
   I heard Thy Majesty confessed,
   For I was with the crowds that pressed
Around that gaunt and shaggy form;
The wild ascetic seemed to find

The Temptation.

    In Thee, disciple and successor.
How well he awed the vulgar mind !
    And has he made Thee a possessor
Of all his walletful of charms,
Persuasions backed by strange alarms?
An Alexandrian Jew you see,
    Revisiting the ancient home,
Feel no surprise to find in me
    The venial faults of those who roam ;
Within our city bounds there meet
    The dwellers of a hundred climes ;
One hears the subtle Gentiles treat
    Of vain philosophies at times.
If Thou dost not design deceiving,
Give me a sign for my believing:
Transform these stones, that we may feed,
If Thou art Son of God indeed?

Christ. Thy words are true ; I am a Son,
    And as a Son I will obey,
    Nor can a miracle be done

Except My Father show the way.
And I must wait for His behest;
 Lift up thy prayer, on Him depending
Each situation seems the best.
 The hunger pangs thy body rending,
At His first utterance shall cease,
And thou shalt taste My bread of peace.

II.

The Edge of a Parapet of the Temple.

Satan (*as a Rabbi*). Why, Master, here alone and
  grave?
The crowds unconscious pass Thee by,
They know not their Messiah; cry,
" Oh, Israel! I am come to save."
Perchance they smile, or will not heed,
 Or gather round with idle jesting,
And even Thou must see the need
 To prove Thy claim by some attesting.
This valley at our feet, behold;

Now Thou art innocent and bold,
Thy Father will not fail Thee, leap,
And we shall see the angels sweep
Around Thy form, in airy bands,
And bear Thee buoyant in their hands;
And all shall wonder at the sight;
  As in the prophecy, we read,
The laws of earth are Thine by right,
  If Thou art Son of God indeed.

Christ. Yea, Son of God, but Son of man,
  My body bound by God's decree,
Nor can I violate His ban,
  To prove my own divinity;
This constant and obedient love,
My highest Sonship is declaring,
  The Lord Himself my claim will prove,
By marvels of His own preparing.

III.

A Mountain Ridge.

Satan (as a Rabbi). From solitude to city life,
 From city back to solitude,
 These vagrant dreams Thy grasp elude ;
Thy vaunted peace is inward strife.
Poor dreamer ! burst the mystic thread
 Which fancy round Thy soul is weaving
Delilah-like ; lift up Thy head,
 Here are new gifts for Thy receiving.
For Thee no stones are changed to bread,
For Thee no angel wings are spread.
I did but test Thine ardent soul,
And offer now a worthier rôle.
The steps of David's throne ascend,
 Those broken steps in kingly guise,
For I Messiah's cause befriend ;
 Spread at Thy feet Thy kingdom lies.
The breath of war Thou shalt not fear,
Nor brazen clash, whilst I am near.

The Temptation.

So shalt Thou gain a royal meed,
If Thou art Son of God indeed.

Christ. These martial dreams of bygone years,
    Like mirror's breath havè passed away;
I ask no throne begirt with spears,
    But wait a wider, nobler sway,
In every land to plant my throne,
O'er loving hearts to rule alone.

Satan. Ambitious Prince ! Thy reign extend,
    With newborn sight I gift Thine eyes,
Before Thee, earth to farthest end,
    And her imperial cities rise ;
Their glory and their power are mine,
    Their changing sceptres in my giving,
And every sceptre shall be Thine,
    The worship of all people living ;
Bow down, on bended knee revere !
No petty Jew Thou see'st here,
But one on whom all power depends,

To share amongst his faithful friends;
So shalt Thou spread Thy gentle creed,
If Thou art Son of God indeed.

Christ. I know thee, Satan.   Get thee gone!
All worship is for God alone.

IV.

At the Foot of the Cross.

Satan (as a Rabbi, passing and repassing). Descend
    and live, Immortal Son,
  Redeem Thy body from the grave,
    As Thou hast savèd others, save
Thyself—in vain Thy course is run.
Here, in Thy last, Thy dying hour,
  Know that the marvels of Thy doing
Were evidences of my power,
  And now too late Thy madness rueing
(Oh, peasant lad of Galilee,
Safe in Thy mock divinity),

Learn all Thy loss through Thy rejection
    Of my rich offers on the hill,
Without the shield of my protection,
    Without my wariness and skill,
I have permitted Thee to fool
Thyself and others, as my tool;
Turn to Thy Father—is He nigh?
He will not leave Thee there to die,
Upon that sinner's cross to bleed,
If Thou art Son of God indeed.

Christ. My God, my God, I cry to Thee—
Why, why hast Thou forsaken me?

II.

A FINE SUNDAY.

White. How all the country moves and stirs!
    A livelier pulse the year time feels;
Birds burst from bush with sudden whirs,
    In sympathy the belfry peals;
It peals the bridal of the spring,
    To-day with summer's lusty prime.
Two larks have caught the notes, and sing
    To fleecy clouds this Sabbath chime;
No valley seems completely fair
    Till God's grey walls within it stand:
See through the trees, the church is there,
    A rock of rest in weary land.

A Fine Sunday.

Black. And see! the ghostly yew-tree stands
  In sable cowl beside the gate;
And downward points its bony hands
  To swelling graves for all that wait.
Death's dragon jaws are always by,
  To scare the young and light away,
With broken headstones, stumps awry,
  And fresh teeth added day by day.
I will not pass my grave to pray
  'Neath spreading tree sure God is near.
By hillside altar let us stay;
  Of common stones our Bethel rear.

White. Ah, yes! I know the story well:
  How much these meditations yield!
Five minutes' thought on heaven and hell,
  Then—profits of a turnip field,
Then—calculations as to kine,
  Or like anxieties begin.
Surrender once your will to mine;—
  I take your arm perforce; come in.
    [*They enter the church.*

Black. But what a change ! This musty chill,
    The sculptured dead, the slabs of brass,
Instead of sunlight on the hill,
    And cowslip patches on the grass !
No lark's song penetrates these walls :
    We have the parson's sleepy tones,
A choir of bumpkins yells and bawls,
    The wheezy organ creaks and groans.

White. Yet there's a gospel in the drone ;
    This music, on its broken wings,
Can soar where never lark has flown,
    And lifts each humble soul that sings,
And think you nature's blind disport
    The great Intelligence can please ?
The faintest sigh from contrite thought
    Is more to Him than summer breeze.

Black. That window, with its coloured saints,
    See ! how the sun is flaming through !
Upon the marble dead he paints

A Fine Sunday.

A gospel scene in red and blue.
And so your weekly gospel comes,
   To stony hearts its picture shows;
The Sunday scholar yawns and hums,
   The old, in reverent posture, doze;
The squires' heads are full of plans;
   Their rivals' dress their daughters eye;
Two rustics, blushing for their banns,
   Chafe as the weary prayers roll by.

White. Well, well, and if I grant you all,
   Some seeds of good may root; who knows?
In any cranny of the wall
   The golden moss and lichen grows:
And none the ways of God can know,
   Or whom His Christ has gained or lost;
On souls unknown His breath may blow,
   And cause a secret Pentecost.

III.

LAW AND LIBERTY.

A Spring Morning. A Valley on the South Coast of England.

Elack. Here, down the rugged pathway leaps
 To yonder terraced shingle shore ;
From daisied bluffs, and primrose steeps,
 The swollen mimic torrents roar ;
And through the valley's wooded maze
 There swiftly threads a steel-bright line,
 To seek the sea, which gives no sign,
Save sighs, beneath grey hood of haze.

Law and Liberty.

The long grass riots at the knee;
   Tall harebells battle for the light;
And budding fern fronds fair to see,
   Curled like the old world ammonite,
Are locked across the path we tread;
   A light mist floats above the trees,
   A golden vapour, which the breeze
Tears into blue rents overhead.

What said you up amongst the hills,
   About the higher Christian life?
On such a day each spirit fills,
   All being with the spring is rife.
A higher life than this reveal?
   With face upturned to Nature's face,
   To mirror every changing grace,
The beating of her heart to feel.

Arch-prophetess of God unknown,
   How fairly He has fashioned thee!
Thou witnesseth for Him, alone,
   His handiwork, not Him, we see.

Great Mother, we are all thy brood ;
    God wrought thee in six days, they say,
    Now keeps His endless Sabbath day ;
From thy kind breasts we draw all good.

Our childhood should be spring's soft day,
    Bright sunlight dimmed by fleeting tears ;
And youth should flush with passion's sway,
    For love should rule the golden years ;
Life's revel for the summer's glow ;
    Discreeter age creeps on too soon,
    With harvest field and autumn moon,
And then—I know not what—the snow.

My friend, the only guide Divine,
    Is Nature's voice without, within,
And why should man her gifts resign,
    And count her touch, her impulse, sin?
And make religion pain and loss?
    The holy man,—the devotee,
    The fakir swinging from his tree,
The Christian with his daily cross?

Law and Liberty.

Come, brother, from monastic grave,
    And in the wholesome daylight dwell.
Come, Puritan, from moral cave,
    For self-denial is not well.
The shadow of the Cross sweeps round
    The darkening Earth, which is bereft
    Of pleasures simpler faiths had left,
And deepens shade wherever found.

White. To Nature's judgment you appeal,
    Then to this Cæsar we will go;
And has she never made us feel
    A thirst for more than she can show,
A longing for the Great Unknown,
    For God, the world beyond our ken?
    We question her in vain, and then
Find we are in the dark alone.

No, not alone does man remain,
    God breaks upon his Arctic night,
And kindles once, and yet again,
    The splendours of the Northern Light

The fitful blaze of prophecy;
    Whilst the fixed stars for guidance glow,
    Pale conscience lights which ever show,
Reflected in the heart's dark sea.

And then amidst the Syrian hills
    A village carpenter appears,
Drops saw and chisel, and fulfils
    A teacher's part for three short years.
And when disciples round Him throng,
    With self-denying doctrines new,
    He winnows out a faithful few,
To bear a heavy cross along.

His words are blown about by fame,
    We feel their gracious influence here,
As Son of God, the peasant's claim,
    And creed of sorrow, still are dear.
For love of God and human kind,
    The Carpenter Himself has wrought
    His cross of sacrifice, and brought
His people to their Master's mind.

Law and Liberty.

How Nature's altars run with blood !
    Her law of sacrifice is seen
Throughout the world in field and flood ;
    The weak receive her sentence keen.
Old types and feebler forms of life
    Before the stronger disappear.
    To reach her own ideal clear,
Serene she wades through blood and strife.

This moral life,—this life of God,
    Fights upwards into air more free,
And underneath its feet are trod
    All that oppose its victory.
Until the power of evil fails ;
    New heavens to new earth unroll ;
    Fair body mates with perfect soul ;
And in both worlds the best prevails.

PSALM AND SONG.

A GIFT.

"A box of ointment . . . . very precious."

SHE brought her box of eastern scents,
  The oil perfumed His feet;
To others 'twas five hundred pence,
  To Him a worship sweet.

The prisoned incense filled the air,
  The box was cast aside,
The winds have borne the fragrance where
  They preach the Crucified.

And who regards the broken jar?
  "Forgotten" is its doom.
The incense shall exhale afar
  From Joseph's garden tomb.

A Gift.

Such gift we, too, would bring to Thee,
   And if the box must break,
Accept the offering thus set free,
   The suffering for Thy sake.

"*SUFFER LITTLE CHILDREN.*"

TO Thee the Hebrew mothers pressed,
    To Thee their children came,
Thy voice the tender infants blessed,
    And put their foes to shame;
They hastened to Thy company;
Thy hands each little form caressed,
And still the children come to Thee.

They come, in vain we bade them stay,
    A voice we could not hear
Had called them from our arms away,
    And, blind with many a tear,

"Suffer Little Children."

We sought for them; we could not see,
We touched Thine arms,—within they lay,
For still the children come to Thee.

Within Thy house the children stand,
   By birthright they appear;
For, passing by the rich and grand,
   Thy text is chosen here;
And learning their humility,
We, too, will join the lowly band,
For only children come to Thee.

Within Thine arms, Thy house, Thy love,
   These little ones how blessed!
They rise on pinions of a dove,
   And enter into rest.
And in their angel purity
Behold the Father's face above,
And still the children come to Thee.

"WHAT THINK YE OF CHRIST?"

THE peasant when he turns to pray,
    Midst snows of Alp or Appenine,
Finds rugged Christ at each crossway,
    Or Virgin with the Doll Divine;
    Far down amidst the trellised vine,
In green depths swings the chapel-bell;
To whom he prays he cannot tell,
He prays for luck, or fear of some ideal hell.

A poor man hears the holy Name
    Oft uttered in the house of prayer,
The house for rich and poor the same,
    And yet the rich are chiefly there;

"What think ye of Christ?"

He meets the Saviour everywhere,
In ghostly marble on the wall,
From painted panes His shadows fall,
The rich man's scant return to Christ who gave him all.

Perchance a woman dreams of Him
    After a lapse of ruined years,
She tries to piece some story dim,
    And murmurs, "Master," through her tears.
    But when no helping voice she hears,
No more of Him she strives to think,
But bids both soul and body sink;—
No shore of Galilee is the dark river's brink.

The man with worldly thought engrossed
    Finds every Christian doctrine clear,
His freedom is his quiet boast,
    From what his wife and girls revere;
    Nor chance of error does he fear.
"The Christ of history we praise
Looms grandly through tradition's haze,
But does not touch our lives in these enlightened days."

"What think ye of Christ?"

The bigot claims Him for his own,
    Within four narrow walls to keep,
He builds the fold for few alone,
    And drives away the other sheep;
    And gauges Christ's compassions deep,
And grudges all in worship found
Beyond the plaster chapel's bound,
Or out of some old minster's hushed and hallowed ground.

Where is the storied Christ of old?
    And where the triumphs of His arm?
Adown the centuries, behold!
    He comes with steady pace and calm;
    Before Him tumult and alarm,
The hoary idols sway and fall,
And selfishness, grey god of all,
Feels the throne shake, and bows his crownéd crest so tall.

Behind Him, in the path He trod,
    New hopes for man, new pleasures spring,
And now the sometime barren sod
    Smiles with a sudden blossoming;

His hands immortal promise bring;
See, on His face there glows a light!
The morning star whose glory bright
Streams from the coming world to quench eternal night.

Go forth, O Lord, to conquer still,
   The sorrowful and sick remain;
Far spreads the ancient realm of ill,
   The kingdoms of disease and pain.
   Take up, at length, Thy power and reign.
Arm us with two-edged sword, we pray,
These enemies of man to slay:
True science and true love will win the better day.

THE WORD OF THE LORD.

"And the word of the Lord was precious in those days; there was no open vision."

"'Ere the lamp of God went out in the temple of the Lord, . . . the Lord called Samuel."

WHENE'ER the lamp of God is burning low,
    When fails the warning voice of prophecy,
  Upon the waning flame about to die,
Anon the Spirit of the Lord will blow,
A vision unto childlike hearts will show.
    But let the prophet's muster-roll be read,
    No voice will answer from the mighty dead,
  No more Elias can his robe bestow.
They hold their peace;—the very stones cry out,

The ancient rocks their hidden tale reveal,
The stars and seas their mysteries unseal.
But seers and sons of science, both we doubt ;
" Behold these dreamers come," we mocking say.
God send us truth, come from what source it may.

MORNING.

A MOMENT'S thought we give Thee now,
    The morning's first-fruits yield,
Before our hands are on the plough,
    Or feet are in the field.

The paths of life run hard by death,
    Our heedless footsteps guide;
Thou Carpenter of Nazareth,
    Toil ever by our side.

When in the noontide heat and care,
    Earth, earth alone we see,
Teach us at noon with silent prayer
    To turn and look on Thee.

Morning.

Endow our hands with hearty skill,
    To labour at our best,
And when the work exceeds our will,
    Take up, O Lord, the rest.

If sin approach, and we reject
    The ploughshare for the sword,
Rebuke the tempter, and protect
    Our souls, all-conquering Lord.

Before the tongue's unruly gate
    Bid some good angel stay,
And may Thy patient Spirit wait,
    To cleanse our thoughts all day.

EVENING.

I.

NOW from the world we turn away,
    As one by one its voices cease,
Lord, at the closing of the day,
    Stand in our midst and breathe Thy peace.

Create in every wearied breast
    A quiet garden,—dewy place,
A little paradise of rest,
    Where God at eventide may pace.

Each spirit walking by Thy side,
    In nakedness, but not with shame,
No longer seeking sin to hide,
    Shall listen to Thy righteous blame.

Thy swift forgiving love shall learn,
    And from Thy wisdom counsel take,
From daily fault and failure turn,
    To strive anew for Thy dear sake.

Then till Thy goodness shall restore
    The priceless gifts of light and sun,
Give from Thy perfect treasure store
    The sleep of Thy belovéd one.

II.

"For so he giveth his beloved sleep."

THOU Giver of a perfect peace,
    Proclaim a truce to sorrow;
Bid all our care and trouble cease,
    Until the coming morrow.

Evening.

Stay by the hot and fevered head,
    Stay by the couch of weeping,
Until a calm broods o'er the bed,
    And Thy beloved are sleeping.

Rebuke the shades of ancient sin
    By which our souls are daunted,
Lest by old follies trooping in
    Our midnights should be haunted.

We oft renew the strife of day,
    The night a battle making,
And bind our armour for the fray
    Before the morn is breaking.

From all this fruitless toil we turn,
    From barren watches keeping,
The victors in the strife, we learn,
    Are Thy belovéd, sleeping.

Evening.

The gift of happy rest is Thine,
   For those in Thee confiding,
Bestow the perfect anodyne,
   The peace of God abiding.

ADVENT.

I.

The Preaching of St. John the Baptist.

SAVIOUR, wake a voice to-day,
As of old to smooth Thy way,
In the wilderness to cry,
In these hearts so hard and dry;
Till we turn from earthly care,
Startled by the loud "Prepare!"
Till we haste Thy word to hear,
Quickened by a sudden fear.

"Lo, Thy kingdom is at hand,"
Lord we hear, and trembling stand;
Dost Thou not within us see
Something of the Pharisee?

Advent.

Violence or fraud within,
Publican or soldier's sin?
Bid the piercing desert cry,
Search these crowded thoughts and try.

Sinful soilings washed away,
We will hail Thy coming sway;
Meek and lowly wilt Thou come,
Stable for Thy palace home?
Single star for diadem,
Pendent over Bethlehem?
Angels singing lullaby,
Simple shepherds wondering by?

Thou wilt come with pomp Divine,
On the sky Thy blazoned sign;
Earth shall heave with quickened dead,
Song resound and wail of dread;
Throned on cloud our King will be,
Every eye His glory see;
With the royal white-winged throng
May we raise the gladsome song.

II.

O LORD, "how long," Thy people cry,
    The sons of God, in phalanx deep,
Keep patient watch as years roll by,
    Whilst heaven is calm and graveyards sleep.

They wait Thy march with eager eyes,
    And on their lips hosannas wait;
Whilst sin sends up its scoffing cries,
    Creation groans disconsolate.

But yoke them to Thy kingly car,
    To hasten that triumphal day,
For all Thy burdens easy are,
    And very gentle is Thy sway.

Command the loud archangel's blast
    To wake the dead, the clouds unroll;
Thy scattered family at last
    From heaven and earth shall gather whole.

III.

"And I will give him the morning star."

LORD JESUS of the cross and thorn,
    With many crowns exalted now,
Still is Thy cross by Christians borne,
    Thy thorns surround each servant's brow;
But all our pains remembered are,
Lord Jesus of the sword and star.

Forth from Thy mouth the sword proceeds,
    Thy voice is august as the sea;—
For succour in His people's needs,
    The Lord a man of war will be;—
Thy morning promise burns afar,
Lord Jesus of the sword and star.

In darkness Thou wilt come to aid;
    Although our souls are tempest-tossed,
The star of morning rides the wave,
    With guiding light for spirits lost;
We safely cross death's stormy bar,
    Lord Jesus of the sword and star.

Advent.

We pray Thee for Thy peace, the rest,
    The world can neither make nor mar;
But above other gifts, the best,
    Thy herald bright the morning star;
Then heaven's fair daybreak is not far,
Lord Jesus of the sword and star.

CHRISTMAS.

THE Lord is moved to pity,
　By earth's sad cries and tears;
And now in David's city,
　Immanuel appears;
For whom through weary ages
　The wise have waited long;
For whom the prophet sages
　Have prayed in burning song.

Christmas.

The mother to His manger
   Her trembling love-gift brings;
The shepherd and the stranger
   Adore with gifts of kings;
The highest heavens are sending
   Bright angels from afar;
And midnight skies are bending
   With music and a star.

And still Thy servants offer
   Their richest gifts to Thee;
The mighty masters proffer
   Their wealth of poesy;
For Thee the poems living,
   In stone and canvas shine,
All honour to Thee giving,
   Thou royal Babe Divine.

And still Thy servants offer
   Such service as they may;
Some cast into Thy coffer,
   And some can only pray;

Christmas.

And some may shed as treasure
   Their blood on pagan spears;
And some in patience measure
   Their martyrdom by years.

Within the royal stable
   We come with good intent;
But little are we able
   With others to present;
No mighty work or token,
   No gold or costly gem;
But sinful hearts and broken,
   O Babe of Bethlehem.

FOR LENT.

OUR Saviour held a hidden life
   Amidst our worldly din;
Athwart the course of daily strife,
   He brought a silence in.

Alone the mountain path He trod,
   To seek a place to pray;
In solitude He met with God,
   And in a desert way.

For Lent.

And in our lives' tumultuous round
    Of mingled joy and care,
Is there no quiet mountain found,
    For holy thought and prayer?

No calm retreat in which to hide,
    The inmost heart's recess?
No fast from earthly pomp and pride,
    With Christ in wilderness?

For if no resting-place is found,
    The Lord will interpose,
Make barren all our pleasant ground,
    Till deserts round us close.

And then we find the stillness best
    For penitence and prayer;
We enter into needful rest,
    And meet our Father there.

PALM SUNDAY.

COME down, anointed King,
    The royal city waits;
Thy courts with children's praises ring,
    Thy people throng the gates.

Thine army on the hill
    With palms and songs rejoice;
And stolid stones have felt the thrill,
    And almost found a voice.

Palm Sunday.

A robe Thy people find;
   A crown of thorns they weave;
A throne of wood, and nails to bind
   The King they now receive.

Why tarries yet the King?
   Why rests He on the hill?
Whilst songs are changed to wondering,
   And waving palms are still.

But careless of the cry,
   The loud exulting cheers;
He casts the palms of triumph by,
   And strews His path with tears.

And do the cross and shame
   Provoke this sudden woe?
Nay, but He views the sword and flame
   Lay rebel Salem low.

Palm Sunday.

Nay, but His brooding love
    O'er earth would spread its wing;
And all His deep compassions move
    At her sad wandering.

Come down, anointed King.!
    Come not with songs, but sighs;
Our grief and sympathy we bring,
    Our pealing triumph dies.

This is Thy royal course,
    With tears and blood 'tis stained;
We follow to Thy throne the cross,
    And see the kingdom gained.

And soon shall every knee
    Be bowed in worship true;
With singing we shall see with Thee
    Jerusalem the New.

GOOD FRIDAY.

LORD, is there room beneath Thy cross for me,
    Where mourners lie,
  Where strangers marvel at Thine agony,
    And scoffers cry?
  Here let me find amidst the crowd a place,
  To watch the awful changes on Thy face.

  We see the look of love which conquers pain,
    The filial care;

Good Friday.

That gives the mother back a son again;
    And hear the prayer,
Forgive them; to a dying sinner's sigh,
    The gates of Paradise asunder fly.

But soon the deadly pain all conquering grows;
    I thirst, He calls;
The earth beneath us shares His dying throes;
    The noontide palls;
Yet on His visage deeper shadows lie,
Betoken that a darker change is nigh.

It comes; the sun is black with sudden clouds,
    Earth throbs with fear;
And lo! the holy dead forsake their shrouds
    As He draws near;
In haste the reverent host forsake the gloom,
Soon as the Ever-living seeks the tomb.

His Father's face is lost in midnight veil,
    To God, He cries;

The crowd in silence hear His dying wail;
He bows and dies;
He dies, the parting veil is rent in twain,
He enters to His Father's face again.

EASTER.

THE day is come which vanquished night;
    The captive King of kings is free;
When flower-crowned forth from dark to light
    Leaped life and immortality.

No need of spice, or tears, or sighs,
    For angel hands have been before;
And Love has dried her wondering eyes
    Before the tomb with open door.

Easter.

We sing of empty graves to-day,
    Of death who takes, but cannot keep;
And see the place where Jesus lay,
    Wherever our belovéd sleep.

With faltering steps we reach the place,
    What can we through the gloom descry?
An angel sits with smiling face,
    With finger lifted to the sky.

Yes, white-winged faith reveals alone
    To faithful souls this bright surprise;
Lord, Thou canst roll away the stone,
    This stony doubt which seals our eyes.

Come gracious Gardener, to-day,
    By tear-blind Marys ever seen;
Both we and our belovéd, say,
    Shall wake within a garden green.

ASCENSION DAY.

PSALM XXIV.

ABOVE the world there rises high
　The mountain of the Lord;
"Oh, who may enter in," I cry,
　"To see the face of God?"
"For pure in heart is this abode,"
　I hear a voice reply;
All silent is that mountain road,
　For no man passes by.

Ascension Day.

Who breaks the silence of the place
    With trump and martial din?
The King of glory comes apace,
    And He must enter in.
Before the gate His heralds see!
    But from the heights they say,
Who may this King of glory be,
    To whom we should give way?

And know you not the Lord our King?
    The Lord of hosts is He;
From distant lands His armies bring
    The spoils of victory.
His robes are red with battle stains,
    His feet, His hands are marred;
He purchased triumph by His pains,
    And are the portals barred?

Then tremble all the doors and shake
    The gates with thunder loud,
Our King doth first His entrance make,
    And after throngs a crowd;

Ascension Day.

A captive crowd His triumph grace,
    Redeeméd from the foe,
And pure in heart to seek His face,
    Throughout the mount they go.

WHITSUNDAY.

WILL God most holy come again,
    As in the ancient days?
We seek His house, but seek in vain
    The dread Shekinah blaze.

Will God most holy deign to dwell
    With man in garb of clay?
He came, He tasted death and hell,
    But Christ has passed away.

Whitsunday.

We gather in His holy place,
    And pray for times of old;
The pure in heart would see His face,
    Ere love and hope are cold.

Come, Lord, and magnify Thy name,
    Whilst eager eyes are dim,
With sound of wings and tongues of flame,
    Come throned on cherubim.

He comes, his mighty pinions sweep,
    A rushing wind before;
Our souls, His temples, silence keep,
    His breath unseals the door.

And God descends with man to dwell,
    For ever to abide;
Let tongues of flame this gospel tell,
    Like lightnings far and wide.

TRINITY SUNDAY.

WHO can know Thee, God of might?
   Who can pierce Thy shrine of light?
Lovers of the world, indeed,
May repeat a careful creed.
Many gather at Thy throne,
   Who Thy presence cannot see;
To the pure in heart alone
   Happy vision comes of Thee.

Trinity Sunday.

Not for any land or race
Only shines Thy gracious face;
Not within Thy Church's bound
Only is Thy glory found.
Holy living Thou wilt own,
    Faulty though the faith may be;
To the pure in heart alone
    Happy vision comes of Thee.

All the truth from Thee must flow,
Nothing of ourselves we know;
Vain our thought, our knowledge vain,
Wise men lose and children gain;
Keep us watchful at Thy gate,
    From the world's defilement free;
Unto humble souls that wait,
    Happy vision comes of Thee.

Glory to our Christ, the Son,
Manhood with the Godhead One;
By His Spirit doth He still
Earth with His dear presence fill.

Trinity Sunday.

God in Christ may they adore,
    Who can pierce no mystery;
To the simple without lore
    Happy vision comes of Thee.

A CHILD'S MORNING HYMN.

OUR Father, all Thy children bless,
    Bless us this morn, we pray;
Thy hands have spun the lily's dress,
    Thy hands clothe us to-day.
To Thee the hungry ravens cry,
    And none unheeded fall;
We too are guarded by Thine eye,
    And Thou hast food for all.

A Child's Morning Hymn.

The world so wide with work is filled,
    To us our duty show;
Above, the feathered toilers build,
    The busy ants below.
The sun is passing through the land,
    And man to labour calls;
Teach us our task with head or hand,
    Before the darkness falls.

For many little ones we pray
    Who never hear Thy name;
Kind Father, pity them alway,
    In homes of sin and shame.
When like the fledgling birds they cry,
    In hunger and distress,
Good angels then are passing by,
    And Thou art near to bless.

A CHILD'S CHRISTMAS CAROL.

CHILD CHRIST, enthroned with glory high,
    But once so meanly born,
O listen to the children's cry
    On this Your holy morn.

A child, to come to You we dare,
    And pray with You to live;
For this Your scarlet wounds You wear,
    What can Your children give?

Their blood, whilst Rachel mother weeps,
  Her little martyr throng;
And once again on Olive's steeps
  They give the palm and song.

Though not with shepherd and with king
  Can we our homage raise,
And gold and spice we may not bring,
  We yet may bring our praise.

So hear us in the golden place,
  • Midst prostrate cherubim,
Where children's angels see Your face,
  Lord, listen to our hymn.

And up to You may we be led,
  To wear the garments white;
The path which all as children tread,
  Who enter in aright.

And now in white will we array,
  Like snow-flakes born of heaven;
The Saviour Child will lead the way,
  And head His band forgiven.

The earth will whiten as we go,
  The Church will bid us speed;
It was Your last command below,
  That she the lambs should feed.

And when we cast life's burdens down,
  To rest with You above,
We'll sing the Manger and the Crown,
  The story of Your love.

So on this day we join the strain
  That angels' voices make,
For if from "glory" we refrain,
  The stones would silence break.

Through angels' voices first we know
When midnight skies are riven;
"To God be praise, to man below
Be peace and pardon given."

BAPTISM.

SOFTLY o'er little faces flow
   The pure, symbolic waves;
Freely Thy Spirit will bestow,
   The grace from sin that saves.
Lord, when Thy trumpet call is heard,
   And world and flesh array,
May all of these young hearts be stirred
   To fight for Thee that day.

Baptism.

The holy sign alone is here,
    Long will the baptism be;
May they through every coming year
    Be buried, Lord, with Thee.—
Baptized into Thy death from sin,
    Each day from self more free,
A daily resurrection win,
    And triumph, Lord, with Thee.

HOLY COMMUNION.

I.

"Lord, evermore give us this bread."

LORD JESUS, feed us evermore,
    Thy body break, Thy blood outpour;
The Christ is dead, His flesh is bread,
We take, and never hunger more.

Lord Jesus, all the feast is Thine,
Thyself impart with bread and wine;
The Christ He lives, His flesh He gives,
And with that food a strength Divine.

Holy Communion.

Lord Jesus, for Thy holy sake
This feast a memory we make;
The Christ will come to take us home,
Until that day His bread we break.

Lord Jesus, to these hearts appear,
Regard Thy fainting people here;
The Christ is good, He gives us food,
And with that food His presence dear.

II.

SPARE me, Holy Master, spare,
    Fragments of the children's fare;
Though unworthy of the meal,
Bowed with sinfulness I kneel;
Lift my empty hands in fear,
Doubting, trembling to be here.

But I see an outstretched hand,
" Eat ye all," is Thy command.

Holy Communion.

Bread of Life, I take of Thee,
By Thy Spirit enter me;
Bruised Vine, a fountain give,
Whereof I may drink and live.

CHRISTIAN MISSIONS.

GOD had apostles from the morn
When first the race of man was born;
On sin to show His anger dread,
The sea arose from rocky bed—
The stormy billows thundered loud,
But mercy's bow o'erspanned the cloud;
Now spring birds sing each vernal calm,
And harvests bend with rustling psalm.

Christian Missions.

God's great Apostle is His Son;
God's love He brought to every one;
But Earth refused the gracious Guest
A transient home or place of rest.
Some fishers offered worship meet;
Some sinful women kissed His feet;
These few, believing on His name,
Redeemed humanity from shame.

God sent apostles far and wide,
To preach the Saviour crucified;
In vain they cried to heedless ears,
And martyrs taught by blood and tears.
Of every thing they suffered loss,
To lift on high that rugged cross;
Till in its shade the weak prevailed,
And every heathen altar paled.

God for His new apostles waits;
O enter we His temple gates,
With willing zeal our hearts inspire,
And touch our lips with coal of fire.

Bestow the apostolic keys,
To bind for Thee, from sin to ease;
To strangers, friends, at home, abroad,
Make us Thy new apostles, Lord.

THE BUILDING OF A NEW CHURCH.

OF old all earth was hallowed ground,
   Thy servant, Lord, of old,
A house of God, a Bethel found,
   Amidst the stony wold.
And yet again Thy presence came
   To temple and to tent;
Thy Spirit with His breath of flame,
   A cloud of fire was sent.

For Thee a dwelling-place we raise;
    Unveil Thy presence here;
In answer to our prayer and praise,
    In glorious form appear.
Resplendent in Thy servants' sight,
    To contrite hearts revealed,
The careless miss Thy glory bright,
    The sinful eyes are sealed.

This earthly dwelling will not last,
    How can we build for Thee?
Eternity, a temple vast,
    Thine only house can be.
The stars are dust beneath Thy feet,
    The shining worlds decay;
Where will the Lord Eternal meet
    His creatures of a day?

Christ, Thy creating hands alone
    The holy house can build;
Thy quarry is the living stone,
    The hearts Thy grace has filled.

The Building of a New Church.

> From age to age the walls divine
>   Are rising firm and well:
> Unite us in Thy great design,
>   Then, Lord, descend and dwell.

THE POOL OF BETHESDA.

FOR THE COMMENCEMENT OF PUBLIC WORSHIP.

BEHOLD a multitude appear,
   Of helpless ones and weak,
Sin-stricken souls, dear Lord, are here,
   Thy living truth they seek.

In vain in streams of truth we lave,
   No health Thy word can bring,
Until Thine angel smite the wave
   With sweep of healing wing.

The Pool of Bethesda.

Not peace, we pray, but send us storm,
  A conscience-stirring hour;
In round of rites, in frequent form,
  We find no quickening power.

Yet more we pray, Thyself to come,
  With healing to Thy hem;
Then leap the lame, then sing the dumb,
  And we will sing with them.

FOR THOSE AT SEA IN STORM.

OUR thoughts go down into the deep,
    When tempests are abroad;
Within an ark of safety keep
    Seafaring souls, good Lord.

These men 'Thy wondrous march behold
    Along the troubled way;
The billows bear Thee as of old,
    The stormy winds obey.

For those at Sea in Storm.

Deep calls to deep, the grand refrain
    Repeats from sea to sky;
He speaks, and ocean's voice again
    Is soothed into a sigh.

O Christ, Thy promises fulfil;
    From the eternal shore
Proclaim a lasting " Peace, be still ! "
    And sea shall be no more.

The crystal waves shall never break;
    The world's unrest is done;
The only sea a burnished lake,
    Beneath the heavenly Sun.

THE SOWER.

GREAT Sower, through my heart I pray,
    Free fling the golden grain;
And in this field make long delay,
    To sow, and sow again.

From sudden swoop of evil wings
    The holy seed-thoughts shield;
And water from Thy heavenly springs
    This hard unthankful field.

The Sower.

And if a weak untimely blade
   At noontide cannot stand,
O Lord, extend a saving shade,
   The shelter of Thy hand.

The harmful weed, the thorn destroy,
   And bless the fruitful sod,
Until I garner in with joy
   To harvest home of God.

THE BURDEN-BEARER.

LO, Thy hands are full of cares,
    Lord, the weary sinner's Friend;
For how many burdened prayers
    Out of broken hearts ascend!
And Thy hands have gathered all,
    And Thy brother's heart is sore:
Dare we still upon Thee call?—
    Bring Thee daily burdens more?

The Burden-bearer.

Not the heavy load we bring,
   But the daily fret and wear;
Little biting thorns that spring
   With the good seed growing there.
But these myriad angry foes
   Stifle grace and good intent;
Gather them, and give repose,
   Master, ere our strength is spent.

In Thy higher light serene,
   Trivial are our troubles here;
All the coming days are seen,
   That to us so dark appear.
From the land where sorrows cease,
   From the home where Thou dost live,
Send our heritage of peace,
   Peace of God, Thy promise, give.

EMMAUS.

I TURN to Thee, dear Son of God,
   When overwhelmed with grief and care,
When, standing by the broken sod,
   I see my loved one hidden there;
Then here I find no resting-place,
But, restless, turn to seek Thy face.

The world goes by with pomp and show;
   I start to seize some glittering prize;

Emmaus.

But on a fruitless quest I go,
   Or, gained, 'tis worthless in mine eyes.
Then nothing here I care to own,
My treasure-trove Thyself alone.

And must I stay for sorrow's night,
   Till friend is false and hopes dispel,
And never seek Thee in the light,
   Or when my life is going well?
And miss Thy counsels kind and wise,
The timely warnings from Thine eyes.

No, let my daily progress prove
   A walk Emmaus-ward with Thee,
And far away the end remove
   That parts me from Thy company;
Or let Emmaus be the goal
Where I shall render up my soul.

And then the world, with noise and strife,
   Shall roll in vain on every side;

Serene shall be my hidden life,
    A long cool walk at eventide;
For only in such calm we hear
Thy holy voice, subdued and clear.

THE ATONEMENT.

LORD, in Thy life, an altar stood,
 Where Thou didst sacrifice each day;
The highest stone is stained with blood,
 Whereon Thy perfect offering lay.

Thou Elder Brother of our race,
 For all our sins Thou didst atone,
And offered up, in Adam's place,
 A life obedience of Thine own.

The Atonement.

By daily course of self denied,
    Thou didst ascend each stony stair,
Then, at the summit, bowed and died,
    And sealed with blood obedience there.

Lord, in our lives high altars stand,
    Where we should sacrifice each day;
And from Thy wounded heart and hand
    Comes strength to help us to obey.

We shall invoke Thy death in vain
    Unless to sin we daily die;
Help us, upon Thy cross of pain,
    The sinful flesh to crucify.

But when each altar-flame has died,
    Each daily sacrifice is done,
We cry, with self dissatisfied,
    " Father, behold Thy perfect Son!"

THE GOODLY FELLOWSHIP OF THE PROPHETS.

PSALM XIX.

LORD, Thy glory and Thy grace,
    Succeeding days proclaim ;
These messengers in every place
    Repeat Thy holy name.

The speechless night would still Thy fame
    On sable scroll declare,
And distant nations spell Thy name
    In shining letters there.

Nor does the sun forbear to teach
  The wonders of Thy hand;
Apostle bright, whose tidings reach
  The most benighted land.

And since our eyes will not believe
  These messages divine,
Thine uttered word our ears receive
  By long prophetic line.

From lip to lip, from age to age,
  The burning message flies;
On peasant, poet, shepherd, sage,
  The prophet's mantle lies.

Their voices cease, their work is done;
  Thou wilt Thyself record;
Speak in the person of Thy Son,
  Incarnate Word and Lord.

THE IDEAL TEMPLE.

PSALM LXXXIV.

THY house is very dear,
  The holy courts I prize;
Thou, Lord of Zion, hear,
For Thee my spirit sighs.
My fainting spirit longs and cries,
Till Zion on my sight arise.

Thy house is full of song,
The birds have nested there,

The Ideal Temple.

The fearless singers throng
About the portals fair.
My drooping pinions swiftly bear
My soul to join the singing there.

Thy house will soon appear
To those who trust in Thee;
No stormy rain they fear,
No "vale of misery."
The stormy rain a draught shall be,
To strengthen them for gaining Thee.

Thy house is full of light
When Thou art passing by;
The Sun and Shield so bright
Make sin and darkness fly.
But let me at the portal lie,
To see Thy glory passing by.

THE GOOD SHEPHERD.

PSALM XXIII.

GREAT Shepherd, Thou art good,
   For when in barren land,
In vain I seek for food,
   For fountain in the sand ;
Thy love spreads out a meadow fair,
And guides the quiet waters there.

And when with careless feet
   I miss this pleasant scene,

The Good Shepherd.

And faint, in desert heat,
   Cry out for pastures green ;
Thy watchful ear has caught the cry,
I see my Shepherd standing by.

Across my path Death flings
   Cold shades that quench the light,
When lo ! with angels' wings,
   The darkened vale grows white.
Thy rod and staff, my Guide, appear,
And Thou art better than my fear.

And once in stormy fight,
   Beset with foes I fell ;
My Captain put to flight
   The woven ranks of hell.
And in the waste a table rose,
To strengthen me against my foes.

A feast His hands prepare ;
   The overflowing wine,

The balmy oil are there,
　　And every blessing mine.
Thy goodness and Thy mercy make
A Bethel I shall not forsake.

THE UNIVERSAL FATHER.

PSALM CIII.

LORD and Father we will bless,
    Heart and lip shall bless Thy name,
For Thy love and tenderness
    Ever are to us the same.
Daily Thou dost sin forgive,
    Every day new plenty brings;
Yea, when sick, Thou bid'st us live,
    Mount from death on eagles' wings.

The Universal Father.

When transgressions like a pall
    Spread and darkened all the sky,
And we feared Thy wrath would fall,
    For Thine anger waxéd high;
Then the Father's pity strove
    For each child His hands had fed,
From the shining of His love,
    East and west the storm-clouds sped.

Never shall the slave in vain
    'Gainst oppressor lift a prayer;
Thy just eyes behold his pain,
    And a Moses shall be there.
When we raised a trembling cry
    From the circle of our foes,
Then, oh, then the Lord was nigh,
    Awful unto judgment rose.

King of love and glory, hail!
    High we raise triumphant strain,
But our loudest praises fail,
    Angels catch the glad refrain.

Firstborn of the sons of light,
    Veiled in shadow of your wings,
With your much excelling might
    Magnify the King of kings.

THE WATCHFUL PROVIDENCE.

PSALM XCI.

BROOD over me, my God,
  On Thee my spirit calls;
Thy mountain nest shall peace afford,
  For there Thy shadow falls.

Whilst worldly men below
  Run rioting or weep,
God's children pleasant days may know,
  And quiet nights for sleep.

And if they must descend,
    To tread the stony plain,
His shining host their steps defend,
    And waft them home again.

How royally they go
    Aloft on angels' hands;
Beneath their feet the savage foe,
    Secure by God's commands.

When ghastly dangers come,
    The horrors pass them by;
Unharmed they see the sinners' doom,
    The many thousands die.

Lord, set my soul on high,
    In shadowed eyrie hide;
Thy goodness answers to my cry,
    And I am satisfied.

THE ETERNAL PRESENCE.

PSALM CXXXIX.

LORD! I fear Thy piercing gaze,
   I meet Thine eyes on every side,
And secret thought and word and ways,
   All, all in vain I strive to hide.

The beaten track, from day to day,
   Of common toil obscure I tread;
But here Thou dost upon me lay
   Thy sudden hand, a touch I dread.

The Eternal Presence.

O whither shall my spirit fly?
   If I should burst the arch of blue,
And rise above this lower sky,
   Thine awful judgment throne I view.

Or if I seek eternal shade,
   Where Silence mounts her throne, the tomb,
The death and darkness cannot aid,
   Thy voice will echo through the gloom.

Let breezy morning lend her wing,
   Swift, strong, and striped with blue and gold;
Its joyous sweep my soul shall bring
   Beyond the limit of His hold.

Some barren isle, some distant shore,
   Shall yield at length its rest to me;
But no! my God has gone before,
   The solitude is filled with Thee.

The Eternal Presence.

Or wrapped by night in blackest fold,
   I think to keep a hidden way;
When, as to Israel of old,
   God's flaming sheaf turns night to day.

I yield, my Lord, and since Thine eye
   Must pierce to every secret part,
Behold my thoughts, and search, and try,
   And cleanse the fountain of my heart.

Thy thoughts my thankful love shall trace,
   They every waking moment please;
I hold them mirrored from Thy face,
   As stars are held by waveless seas.

THE NEW WORLD.

AROUND this world of gladness
   A boundless ocean rolls;
Its voice is full of sadness,
   A dirge for human souls.
Those bitter waves are freighted
   With goodly company,
And all of earth are fated
   To that eternal sea.

The New World.

We join in passing pleasures,
   And do not hear the sound;
In flow of higher measures
   Those lower notes are drowned;
But when life's strains are finer,
   In pause of harmony
Comes in the mournful minor
   Of that eternal sea.

Our friends are passing,—whither?
   We never see them more,
No voices are borne hither
   From yonder unknown shore.
With stormy land-breeze blowing,
   And we from earth cast free,
Oh, guide us, God all knowing,
   O'er that eternal sea.

These voyagers discover
   A new and summer world;
The morning mists that hover
   Around it shall be furled.

No longer shall be holden,
    From eyes that look to Thee,
The heavenly Indies golden,
    Of that eternal sea.

FOR TIME OF TEMPTATION.

A SILENT battle-field;
    No cry of war or woe;
But shivered sword, abandoned shield,
    The daily conflict show.

Alone each soldier stands,
    Begirt with deadly foes;
Yet targe and sword-blade in his hands
    Re-echo not the blows.

For Time of Temptation.

Unknown the mighty fall,
    Their shield is cast away;
And feeble souls surrender all,
    Nor yet for succour pray.

But when the valiant cry
    For succour to the Lord,
A golden glory from the sky
    Gilds battered helm and sword.

Their foes, in sore amaze,
    Are dazzled by the glow;
And ministering angels raise
    The wounded, stricken low.

Take heart, beleaguered soul,
    Defy thy foes awhile,
Apart the frowning clouds shall roll,
    Pierced by thy Father's smile.

For Time of Temptation.

Thy bruised and dinted mail
   Sufficient is for thee;
The broken sword-blade shall not fail
   To win a victory.

FOR TIME OF SICKNESS.

THOU Man of sorrows, hast Thou known
    Our human flesh, with all its pain?
Yea, Saviour, round Thy head remain
The scar-prints of the crown of thorn.

Before Thy feet, in ancient days,
    The stricken of the land were spread;
A word, a touch, the sick, the dead,
Leaped in Thy train with songs of praise.

For Time of Sickness.

A band of courtiers girt Thee round;
   The sad and sinful sought Thy face;
   So close they pressed, there was no place
For any whole or perfect found.

Here in Thy path myself I cast,
   Here to Thy healing robe I press,
   Lord Jesus, look on my distress,
Unseen in silence go not past.

The keys of life and death are Thine,
   Restore my soul, and yet Thy will
   Alone be done, my spirit fill
With quiet trust in love divine.

If there should come a darker day,
When thought of God is lost in pain,
Then let my helpless spirit gain
Thine everlasting arms, I pray.

FOR THE HOUR OF DEATH.

ALL my past belongs to Thee,
And from sin and misery
Thou hast set Thy servant free.

All my future with Thee lies,
In the compass of Thine eyes,
In Thy guidance good and wise.

Through the misty dark I go,
But the cloud begins to glow
With the glory Thou wilt show.

For the Hour of Death.

Soft in sleep repose I take,
Till the lights of morning break,
Then beneath Thy smile awake.

www.ingramcontent.com/pod-product-compliance
Lightning Source LLC
Chambersburg PA
CBHW030348170426
43202CB00010B/1298